ALBERT'S BRIDGE
and
IF YOU'RE GLAD I'LL BE FRANK

by the same author

*

published by Faber & Faber

ROSENCRANTZ AND GUILDENSTERN ARE DEAD
THE REAL INSPECTOR HOUND
ENTER A FREE MAN

LORD MALQUIST AND MR. MOON
(*Anthony Blond*)

ALBERT'S BRIDGE

AND

IF YOU'RE GLAD I'LL BE FRANK

Two plays for radio

by
TOM STOPPARD

FABER AND FABER
24 Russell Square
London

First published in 1969
by Faber and Faber Limited
24 Russell Square London WC1
Printed in Great Britain by
Latimer Trend & Co Ltd Plymouth
All rights reserved

SBN (cloth bound edition) 571 08518 0
SBN (paperback edition) 571 09037 0

*All professional inquiries in regard to this play shall be addressed
to Fraser & Dunlop (Scripts) Ltd, 91 Regent Street, London W1*

© 1969 by Tom Stoppard

Albert's Bridge received its first production on the BBC Third Programme on the 13th July 1967. The cast was as follows:

BOB	Nigel Anthony
CHARLIE	Alexander John
DAD	Geoffrey Wincott
ALBERT	John Hurt
CHAIRMAN	Victor Lucas
DAVE	Ian Thompson
GEORGE	Anthony Jackson
FITCH	Ronald Herdman
MOTHER	Betty Hardy
FATHER	Alan Dudley
KATE	Barbara Mitchell
FRASER	Haydn Jones

Produced by Charles Lefeaux

If You're Glad, I'll Be Frank received its first production on the BBC Third Programme on 8th February 1966. The cast was as follows:

1ST PORTER	Brian Hewlett
MYRTLE TRELAWNEY	Isabel Rennie
MR. MORTIMER	Henry Stamper
MR. COURTENAY-SMITH	Noel Howlett
SIR JOHN	Alan Haines
LORD COOT	Austin Trevor
BERYL BLIGH	Eva Haddon
OPERATOR	Elizabeth Proud
IVY, a bus conductress	Barbara Mitchell
2ND PORTER	Henry Stamper

Produced by John Tydeman

ALBERT'S BRIDGE

Fade up bridge, with painting on mike. Four men are painting a big girdered railway bridge. They are spaced vertically, in ascending order: BOB, CHARLIE, DAD, ALBERT. *To begin with, the mike is at* ALBERT'*s level, the top.*

BOB (*the most distant*): Char-lee!

CHARLIE (*less distant*): Hel-lo!

BOB: Right Charlie?

CHARLIE: Right! Comin' down! . . . Hey, Dad!

DAD (*an older man, not very distant*): Hel-lo!

CHARLIE: Bob 'n' me is done down here!

DAD: Right!

CHARLIE: Have you done?

DAD: Comin' down! . . . Albert! Al-bert!

CHARLIE (*more distant*): Albert!

BOB (*most distant*): Al-bert!

ALBERT (*very close, crooning softly, tunelessly amid various tunes while painting*):
How high the moon in June?
how blue the moon when it's high noon
and the turtle doves above
croon out of tune in love
saying please above the trees
which when there's thunder you don't run under
—those trees—
'cos there'll be pennies fall on Alabama
and you'll drown in foggy London town
the sun was shi-ning . . . on my Yiddisher Mama.

BOB (*most distant*): Albert!

CHARLIE (*less distant*): Albert!

DAD (*off*): Albert!

ALBERT: Hel-lo!

7

DAD: Bob 'n' me 'n' Charlie's done!

ALBERT: Right!

Dip-brush-slap-slide-slick, and once again, dip, brush, slap—oh, it goes on so nicely . . . tickle it into the corner, there, behind the rivet. . . . No one will see that from the ground; I could cheat up here. But I'd know; so dip, brush, slap, slide and once again for the last time till the next time—every surface sleek, renewed—dip, brush, slap, slick, tickle and wipe—right in there with the old rust-proof rust-brown—all glossed and even, end to end—the last touch—perfection! (*Painting stops.*) Oh my! I could stand back to admire it and fall three hundred feet into the sea. Mind your heads! (*Laughs. Climbing down.*) Mind your head, Dad!

DAD: I'm not your dad. Keep off the wet—work down the slope to the middle—and watch your feet.

(*Everyone climbing down, the distance between them closing.*) Going down for good, oh yes, I'm not facing that again. Ten coats I've done, end to end, and now I'm done all right. I had ambitions, you know. . . .

CHARLIE (*nearer*): Mind my head, Dad.

DAD: Watch my feet, Charlie—comin' down——

CHARLIE: I'll watch your feet—you mind my head. Watch your head, Bob——

BOB (*nearer*): Watch your feet, Charlie——

CHARLIE: Mind my feet Bob—watch my head, Dad. . . .

DAD: I'm not your dad, and mind my feet—that's my head, Albert.

ALBERT: Comin' down. . . . Doesn't she look beautiful?

DAD: Looks the same as always. There's no progress. Twenty years, twenty thousand pots of paint . . . yes, I had plans.

CHARLIE: I thought we'd never see the end of it.

BOB: It's not the bleeding end.

CHARLIE: There's no end to it.

DAD: Ten coats non-stop, one after the other, and it's no improvement, no change even, just holding its own against the weather—that's a long time, that's a lot of paint. I could have made my mark.

8

ALBERT: Continuity—that's hard to come by.

DAD: I've spread my life over those girders, and in five minutes I could scrape down to the iron, I could scratch down to my prime.

ALBERT: Simplicity—so . . . contained; neat; your bargain with the world, your wages, your time, your energy, your property, everything you took out and everything you put in, the bargain that has carried you this far—all contained there in ten layers of paint, accounted for. Now that's something; to keep track of everything you put into the kitty, to have it lie there, under your eye, fixed and immediate—there are no consequences to a coat of paint. That's more than you can say for a factory man; his bits and pieces scatter, grow wheels, disintegrate, change colour, join up in new forms which he doesn't know anything about. In short, he doesn't know what he's done, to whom.

DAD: Watch your feet, Albert. Mind your head, Charlie.

CHARLIE: You mind my head. Take care my feet, Bob——

BOB: Watch your feet, Charlie——

CHARLIE: Mind your feet, Dad——

DAD: That's my head, Albert——

ALBERT: Coming down. . . .

Ah, look at it up there, criss-crossed and infinite, you can't see where it ends—I could take off and swing through its branches screaming like a gibbon!

DAD: Mind where you're putting your feet, Albert.

CHARLIE: Watch my head, Dad.

BOB: Train coming, Charlie.

(*Distant train coming.*)

CHARLIE: I've seen it.

BOB (*jumping down on to gravel*): And down.

CHARLIE: Mind where you jump, Dad.

DAD: Seen it.

CHARLIE (*jumping down*): None too soon.

DAD: Train coming, Albert.

ALBERT: I'm with you.

DAD (*jumps down*): Finished.

CHARLIE: Like hell.

BOB: Well, that's another two years behind you.

DAD: A feller once offered me a half share in a very nice trading station in the China Seas. I had it in me.

ALBERT: Mind your toes.

(*He jumps. Climbing down ends. All are now on mike.*)

Now that's a good way to end a day—ending so much else.

CHARLIE: All right for some. Students.

BOB: Slummers.

CHARLIE: Pocket-money holiday lads, oh yes.

ALBERT: One bridge—freshly painted—a million tons of iron thrown across the bay—rust brown and even to the last lick—spick and span, rust-proofed, weather-resistant— perfect!

DAD: Other end needs painting now. A man could go mad.

(*The train arrives and goes screaming past.*)

(*Set* CHAIRMAN *over end of train, cutting bridge.*)

CHAIRMAN: Let us not forget, gentlemen, that Clufton Bay Bridge is the fourth biggest single-span double-track shore-to-shore railway bridge in the world bar none——

DAVE: Hear, hear, Mr. Chairman——

CHAIRMAN: Thank you, Dave—

GEORGE: I've been studying these figures, Mr. Chairman——

CHAIRMAN: Just a moment, George. We've got an amenity here in Clufton, that bridge stands for the whole town, quite apart from the money earned in railway dues——

DAVE: Hear, hear, Mr. Chairman——

CHAIRMAN: Thank you, Dave.

GEORGE: According to the City Engineer's figures, Mr. Chairman——

CHAIRMAN: Just a moment, George. When my grandfather built this bridge he didn't spare the brass—and I for one, as chairman of the Clufton Bay Bridge Sub-Committee— entrusted as we are with the upkeep and responsibility of what is a symbol of Clufton's prosperity—I for one do not begrudge the spending of a few extra quid on a lick of paint.

DAVE: Hear, hear, Mr. Chairman.

CHAIRMAN: Thank you, Dave.

GEORGE: I know it's a symbol of your prosperity, Mr. Chairman, but——

CHAIRMAN: That's a highly improper remark, George. Clufton's prosperity is what I said.

DAVE: Hear, hear, Mr. Chairman.

CHAIRMAN: Thank you, Dave.

GEORGE: My mistake, Mr. Chairman——but if Mr. Fitch's figures are correct——

FITCH (*distinctive voice; clipped, confident; rimless spectacles*): My figures are always correct, Mr. Chairman.

CHAIRMAN: Hear that, George? The City Engineer's figures are a model of correctitude.

DAVE: Hear, hear, Mr. Chairman.

CHAIRMAN: Thank you, Dave.

GEORGE: Then this new paint he's recommending is going to cost us four times as much as the paint we've been using up to now.
(*Pause.*)

CHAIRMAN: Four times as much? Money?

DAVE: Hear, hear, Mr. Chairman.

CHAIRMAN: Just a moment, Dave. I don't think your figures are correct, George. Mr. Fitch knows his business.

GEORGE: What business is he in—paint?

CHAIRMAN: That's a highly improper remark, George—er, you're not in the paint business, are you, Mr. Fitch?

FITCH: No, Mr. Chairman.

CHAIRMAN: No, no, of course you're not. You should be ashamed, George.

DAVE: Hear, hear, Mr. Chairman.

CHAIRMAN: Shut up, Dave. Now what about it, Mr. Fitch—is this right what George says?

FITCH: Well, up to a point, Mr. Chairman, yes. But in the long run, no.

CHAIRMAN: Don't fiddle-faddle with me, Fitch. Does this new-fangled paint of yours cost four times as much as the paint we've got, and if so, what's in it for you?

GEORGE: Hear, hear, Mr. Chairman.

11

CHAIRMAN: Thank you, George.

FITCH: To put the matter at its simplest, Mr. Chairman, the new paint costs four times as much and lasts four times as long.

CHAIRMAN: Well, there's your answer, George. It costs four times as much but it lasts four times as long. Very neat, Fitch—I thought we'd got you there.

GEORGE: What's the point, then?

FITCH: Apart from its silvery colour, Mr. Chairman, which would be a pleasanter effect than the present rusty brown, the new paint would also afford a considerable saving, as you can no doubt see.

CHAIRMAN: Everybody see that? Well, I don't.

GEORGE: Nor do I.

DAVE: Hear, hear, George.

GEORGE: Shut up, Dave.

FITCH: If I might explain, gentlemen. As you know, in common with other great bridges of its kind, the painting of Clufton Bay Bridge is a continuous operation. That is to say, by the time the painters have reached the far end, the end they started at needs painting again.

DAVE: I never knew that!

CHAIRMAN AND GEORGE: Shut up, Dave.

FITCH: This cycle is not a fortuitous one. It is contrived by relating the area of the surfaces to be painted—call it **A**— to the rate of the painting—B—and the durability of the paint—C. The resultant equation determines the variable factor X—i.e. the number of painters required to paint surfaces A at speed B within time C. For example——

CHAIRMAN: E.g.

FITCH: Quite. Er, e.g. with X plus one painters the work would proceed at a higher rate—i.e. B, plus, e.g. Q. However, the factors A and C, the surface area and the lasting quality of the paint remain, of course, constant. The result would be that the painters would be ready to begin painting the bridge for the second time strictly speaking before it needed re-painting. This creates the co-efficient—Waste.

CHAIRMAN: W.

FITCH: If you like. This co-efficient belies efficiency, you see.

CHAIRMAN: U.C. You see, George?

GEORGE: OK, I see.

FITCH: To continue. Furthermore, the value of the co-efficient—Waste—is progressive. Let me put it like this, gentlemen. Because the rate of painting is constant, i.e. too fast to allow the paintwork to deteriorate, each bit the men come to requires re-painting even less than the bit before it. You see, they are all the time catching up on themselves progressively, until there'll come a point where they'll be re-painting the bridge, while it's still wet! (*Pause.*) No that can't be right. . . .

CHAIRMAN: Come to the point Fitch. Wake up, Dave.

DAVE (*waking up*): Hear, hear, Mr. Chairman.

FITCH: To put it another way, gentlemen, that is to say, conversely. With one too few painters—X minus one—the rate of progress goes down to let us say, B minus Q. So what is the result? By the time the painters are ready to start re-painting, the end they started at has deteriorated into unsightly and damaging rust—a co-efficient representing the converse inefficiency.

CHAIRMAN: Pull yourself together, Fitch—I don't know what you're drivellin' about.

GEORGE: In a nutshell, Fitch—the new paint costs four times as much and lasts four times as long. Where's the money saved?

FITCH: We sack three painters.
(*Pause.*)

CHAIRMAN: Ah. . . .

FITCH: You see, to date we have achieved your optimum efficiency by employing four men. It takes them two years to paint the bridge, which is the length of time the paint lasts. This new paint will last eight years, so we only need one painter to paint the bridge by himself. After eight years, the end he started at will be just ready for re-painting. The saving to the ratepayers would be £3,529 15s. 9d. per annum.

13

GEORGE: Excuse me, Mr. Chairman——

CHAIRMAN: Just a moment, George. I congratulate you, Mr. Fitch. An inspired stroke. We'll put it up to the meeting of the full council.

GEORGE: Excuse me——

CHAIRMAN: Shut up, George.

DAVE: Hear, hear, Mr. Chairman.

FITCH: Thank you, Mr. Chairman.

CHAIRMAN: Thank you, Mr. Fitch.

(*Fade.*)

MOTHER: Aren't you getting up, Albert? It's gone eleven. . . . Are you listening to me, Albert?

ALBERT (*in bed*): What?

MOTHER: I'm talking to you, Albert.

ALBERT: Yes?

MOTHER: Yes-what?

ALBERT: Yes, Mother.

MOTHER: That's better. Oh dear, what was I saying?

ALBERT: I don't know, Mother.

MOTHER (*sighs*): I was against that university from the start.

ALBERT: The country needs universities.

MOTHER: I mean it's changed you, Albert. You're thinking all the time. It's not like you, Albert.

ALBERT: Thinking?

MOTHER: You don't talk to me. Or your father. Well, I'm glad it's all behind you, I hope it starts to wear off.

ALBERT: I wanted to stay on after my degree, but they wouldn't have me.

MOTHER: I don't know what you want to know about philosophy for. Your father didn't have to study philosophy, and look where he is, Chairman of Metal Alloys and Allied Metals. It's not as if you were going to be a philosopher or something. . . . Yes, you could have been a trainee executive by now. As it is you'll have to do your stint on the factory floor, philosophy or no philosophy. That university has held you back.

ALBERT: I'll have to get myself articled to a philosopher. . . .

14

Start at the bottom. Of course, a philosopher's clerk wouldn't get the really interesting work straight off, I know that. It'll be a matter of filing the generalizations, tidying up the paradoxes, laying out the premises before the boss gets in—that kind of thing; but after I've learned the ropes I might get a half share in a dialectic, perhaps, and work up towards a treatise. . . . Yes, I could have my own thriving little philosopher's office in a few years.

(*Pause.*)

MOTHER: Would you like to have some coffee downstairs?

ALBERT: Yes.

MOTHER: Yes-what?

ALBERT: Yes please.

(*Pause.*)

MOTHER: I still think it was mean of you not to let us know you had a summer vacation.

ALBERT: I thought you knew. I've had one every year.

MOTHER: You know I've no head for dates. You could have come home to see us.

ALBERT: I'm sorry—there was this temporary job going. . . .

MOTHER: Your father would have given you some money if you'd asked him.

ALBERT: I thought I'd have a go myself.

MOTHER: You'll have to get up now.

ALBERT: It was fantastic up there. The scale of it. From the ground it looks just like a cat's cradle, from a distance you can take it all in, and then up there in the middle of it the thinnest threads are as thick as your body and you could play tennis on the main girders.

MOTHER: Kate will be up in a minute to make the beds.

ALBERT: It's absurd, really, being up there, looking down on the university lying under you like a couple of bricks, full of dots studying philosophy——

MOTHER: I don't want you getting in Kate's way—she's got to clean.

ALBERT: What could they possibly know? I saw more up there in three weeks than those dots did in three years. I saw the context. It reduced philosophy and everything else. I got a

15

perspective. Because that bridge was—separate—complete—removed, defined by principles of engineering which makes it stop at a certain point, which compels a certain shape, certain joints—the whole thing utterly fixed by the rules that make it stay up. It's complete, and a man can give his life to its maintenance, a very fine bargain.

MOTHER: Do you love me, Albert?

ALBERT: Yes.

MOTHER: Yes-what?

ALBERT: Yes please.

(*Cut to a gavel banged on table.*)

MAYORAL VOICE: Number 43 on the order paper, proposal from Bridge sub-committee. . . .

VOICE 1: Move. . . .

VOICE 2: Second.

MAYORAL VOICE: All in favour.

(*Absent-minded murmur of fifty 'Ayes'.*)

Against. (*Pause.*) Carried. Number 44 on the order paper. (*Fade.*)

(*Fade up knock on door off. Door opens.*)

KATE: Oh, I'm sorry, Mr. Albert.

ALBERT: Hello, I was just thinking of getting up.

(*Cut to.*)

BOB: What—by myself? It would take years.

FITCH: Eight years, yes.

BOB: No. I demand a transfer.

FITCH: I thought I'd give you first refusal.

BOB: I want to go back to painting the Corporation crest on the dustcarts.

FITCH: I could fit you in on the magenta.

BOB: On the what?

FITCH: It's one man to a colour nowadays. Efficiency.

(*Cut.*)

CHARLIE: You must be joking.

16

FITCH: It's an opportunity for you.

CHARLIE: I'd go mad. What's it all about?

FITCH: Efficiency.

CHARLIE: I'm not doing that bridge on me tod.

FITCH: It's no more work than before.

CHARLIE: I'd jump off within a month.

FITCH: Oh. Well, we couldn't have that. That would be only one ninety-sixth of it done.

(*Cut.*)

DAD: You mean it's a cheaper way of doing it.

FITCH: More efficient.

DAD: We've been doing a good job.

FITCH: Efficiency isn't a matter of good and bad, entirely. It's a matter of the optimum use of resources—time, money, manpower.

DAD: You mean it's cheaper. I'm an old man.

FITCH: You've got eight years in you.

DAD: It might be my last eight. I haven't done anything yet— I've got a future.

FITCH: Well, I could put you on yellow no-parking lines.

DAD: Yes, all right.

(*Cut.*)

FITCH: . . . But do you have any qualifications?

ALBERT: I've got a degree in philosophy, Mr. Fitch.

FITCH: That's a little unusual.

ALBERT: I wouldn't say that. There were lots of us doing it.

FITCH: That's all very well if you're going to be a philosopher, but what we're talking about is painting bridges.

ALBERT: Yes, yes, I can see what you're driving at, of course, but I don't suppose it did me any harm. Almost everyone who didn't know what to do, did philosophy. Well, that's logical.

FITCH: You're an educated man.

ALBERT: Thank you.

FITCH: What I mean is, you're not the run-of-the-mill bridge painter, not the raw material I'm looking for.

B   17

ALBERT: Well, I did it in the vacation.

FITCH: Yes . . . yes, I did have reports of you. But surely. . . .

ALBERT: I know what you mean, but that's what I want to do.
I liked it. I don't want to work in a factory or an office.

FITCH: Is it the open air life that attracts you?

ALBERT: No. It's the work, the whole thing—crawling round
that great basket, so high up, being responsible for so much
that is so visible. Actually I don't know if that's why I like
it. I like it because I was happy up there, doing something
simple but so grand, without end. It doesn't get away from
you.

FITCH: The intellectual rather than the practical—that's it, is it?

ALBERT: Probably.

FITCH: I'm the same. It's poetry to me—a perfect equation of
space, time and energy——

ALBERT: Yes——

FITCH: It's not just slapping paint on a girder——

ALBERT: No——

FITCH: It's continuity—control—mathematics.

ALBERT: Poetry.

FITCH: Yes, I should have known it was a job for a university
man. . . .

ALBERT: Like me and you——

FITCH: Well, I went to night school myself.

ALBERT: Same thing, different time.

FITCH: That's what I say.

ALBERT: I'm your man, Mr. Fitch.

FITCH: You'll stick to it for eight years, will you?

ALBERT: Oh, I'll paint it more than once.

(*Cut.*)

(*Breakfast in background.*)

FATHER: Now then, Albert, you've had your fun. When I was
your age I'd got six years of work behind me.

ALBERT: Well, I'm starting work now, father.

FATHER: Quite so, but don't think you're going to start at the
top. You'll get there all right in time but you've got to
learn the business first. Is there any more tea, Mother?

18

MOTHER: Ring for Kate, would you, Albert?

ALBERT (*going*): Yes, mother.

MOTHER: That reminds me.

FATHER: You'll start where I started. On the shop floor.

ALBERT (*approach*): Well, actually, Father——

MOTHER: I don't want to sound Victorian, but one can't just turn a blind eye.

ALBERT: What?

FATHER: Yes, I never went in for books and philosophy and look at me now.

MOTHER: I suppose that's the penance one pays for having servants nowadays.

ALBERT: What?

FATHER: I started Metal Alloys and Allied Metals—built it up from a biscuit-tin furnace in the back garden, small smelting jobs for the cycle-repair shop.

MOTHER: I've suspected her for some time and now one can't ignore it. Even with her corset.

ALBERT: Who?

FATHER: You can come in on Monday and I'll hand you over to the plant foreman.

ALBERT: I've already got a job. Actually.

FATHER: You haven't got a job till I give you one.

ALBERT: I'm going to paint Clufton Bay Bridge, starting Monday.

MOTHER: What colour?

ALBERT: Silver.

FATHER: Just a minute——

KATE (*off*): You rang, madam?

MOTHER: More tea, Kate, please.

KATE: Yes, madam.

MOTHER: And a word.

KATE: Yes, madam.

MOTHER: Are you ill?

KATE: No, madam.

MOTHER: I believe I heard you being ill in the bathroom, this morning.

KATE: Yes, madam.

19

MOTHER: And yesterday?

KATE: Yes, madam.

ALBERT: What's the matter, Kate?

KATE: Nothing, Mr. Albert.

MOTHER: Leave this to me. Cook tells me you fainted in the kitchen last week.

KATE: I came over funny.

ALBERT: Kate. . . .

MOTHER: Let's not beat about the bush. Is it the gardener's boy?

KATE: No, madam.

MOTHER: Then who is it?

ALBERT: Who's what?

MOTHER: Well, I'm sorry. You can have a month's wages, of course. You'd better make sure that the young man does the right thing by you.
(*Cut.*)

KATE: I never thought you'd do the right thing by me, Albert.

ALBERT: We'll be all right. It's a nice room.

KATE: Your mum didn't like it.

ALBERT: My mother's got no taste. I'll make a fire.

KATE: And wrap up warm when you go out—it'll be freezing up there.

ALBERT: Only a breeze.

KATE: It'll be ice in a month. If you fell I'd die, Albert.

ALBERT: So would I.

KATE: Don't you ever fall. They shouldn't make it a year-round job. It's dangerous.

ALBERT: No—you don't know how big it is—the threads are like ladders and the cross-pieces are like piers into the sky.

KATE: You hold on tight, for the spring, and the baby.
(*Cut in bridge and painting.*)

ALBERT: Slip, slap, brush, dip, slop, slide, slick and wipe. . . .
In eight years I'll be pushing thirty, and the Clufton Bay Bridge will be a silver bridge—dip-brush, slick, slide, slap without end, I'm the bridge man,

web-spinning silvering spiderman
crawling between heaven and earth on a
cantilevered span,
cat's cradled in the sky . . .
look down at the toy ships
where the sea pounds under toy trains to
toy towns
under my hand.
Am I the spider or the fly?
I'm the bridge man. . . .

The downstairs maid went upstairs to make a bed that I
was in—and suddenly——
(*Cut out bridge. Cut in crying baby.*)

I name this child Albert.

KATE: You can't.

ALBERT: Very well. I name this child Kate.

KATE: Katherine.

ALBERT: Tomorrow wheel her along to the bridge so I can see
you.

KATE: All right. But don't wave, Albert. Don't wave. If you
waved and fell——

ALBERT: I shan't wave.

(*Cut in bridge and painting.*)
Dip brush, dip brush
without end, come rain or shine;
A fine way to spend my time.
My life is set out for me,
the future traced in brown,
my past measured in silver;
how absurd, how sublime
(don't look down)
to climb and clamber in a giant frame;
dip brush, dip brush, slick, slide wipe
and again.
(*Painting stops.*)
I straddle a sort of overflowing gutter on which bathtub

boats push up and down. . . . The banks are littered with various bricks, kiddiblocks with windows; dinky toys move through the gaps, dodged by moving dots that have no colour; under my feet the Triang train thunders across the Meccano, and the minibrick estates straggle up over the hill in neat rows with paintbox gardens. It's the most expensive toytown in the store—the detail is remarkable. But fragile. I tremble for it, half expecting some petulant pampered child to step over the hill and kick the whole thing to bits with her Startrite sandals.

(*Painting.*)

Don't look down,
the dots are looking up.
Don't wave, don't fall, tumbling down a
telescope, diminishing to a dot.
In eight years who will I be?
Not me.
I'll be assimilated then,
the honest working man, father of three—
you've seen him around,
content in his obscurity, come to terms with public truths,
digging the garden of a council house
in what is now my Sunday suit.
I'm okay for fifty years, with any luck;
I can see me climb
up a silver bridge to paint it for the seventh time,
keeping track of my life spent in painting in the colour of
    my track:
above it all.
How sublime
(dip brush, dip brush) silvering the brown.
Which dot is mine?
Don't wave, don't look down.
Don't fall.
(*Cut bridge.*)

KATE: I saw you today.
ALBERT: What was I doing?

22

KATE: Painting, I suppose. Crawling backwards along a cross-piece.

ALBERT: Pulling silver after me. I didn't see you. Or I didn't see which one was you.

KATE: Coming out of the hairdressers. Six and six, I had it cut.

ALBERT: Just goes to show—if you get far enough away, six and sixpence doesn't show, and nor does anything, at a distance.

KATE: Well, life is all close up, isn't it?

ALBERT: Yes, it hits you, when you come back down. How close it all is. You can't stand back to look at it.

KATE: Do you like my hair like this?

ALBERT: Like what? Oh—yes. Do you like mine?

KATE: I got whistled at in the street.

ALBERT: It's always happening to me.

KATE: A lorry driver, at the traffic lights.

ALBERT: They're the worst, I find.

KATE: Oh, Albert. I had the pram with me too.

ALBERT: You look too young for it. Big sister.

KATE: And I cook very nice, don't I?

ALBERT: I'd whistle at you.

KATE: I'd come, if you whistled. I'd give you a wink and say, 'Cheeky!'

ALBERT: Oh, yes—you'd get off with me. No trouble at all. I'd take you down by the canal after the pictures.

KATE: What do you know about it—with your education and all?

ALBERT: Me? I'm a working man.

KATE: You don't have regrets, do you, Albert?

ALBERT: No.

KATE: It wasn't a good bargain, on the face of it.

ALBERT: It depends on what you want.

KATE: Me and the baby. Two rooms and a forty-five hour week, hard work and no advancement.

ALBERT: I'm not ambitious.

KATE: You could have had so much—a white wedding, nice house, an office job with real prospects, the country club ... tennis. ... Yes, you could have had Metal Alloys and Allied Metals—the top job, responsibility, your own office

23

with telephones. . . .

ALBERT: Yes, I'm well out of that.

(*Cut in bridge and painting.*)

Progress. Two lines of silver meeting in an angle bracket—
—and tickle in there behind the rivet—slip slop and wipe
and on we go up the slope.

Does the town look up? Do they all gawp and say to each
other, look at him! How ridiculous he looks up there, so
small, how laughably inadequate. Or do they say, How
brave! One man against the elements! Pitted against so
much!

The lone explorer feeling his way between the iron
crevasses, tacked against the sky by his boots and fingers.
Dots, bricks and beetles.

I could drown them in my spit.

(*Cut bridge, cut in baby's rattle in background.*)

KATE: That isn't nice, Albert.

ALBERT: Spitting?

KATE: Talking like that.

ALBERT: It doesn't represent desire. I'll let them live. I'm only
trying to tell you what it's like.

KATE: I know what it's like. It's painting a girder. There's other
jobs.

ALBERT: It's my bridge—I wish you'd stop her rattling, it's
getting on my nerves.

KATE: That's very advanced for six months.

ALBERT: I'm not doubting her progress. If she played the
trumpet it would be even more advanced but it would still
be sending me round the twist. Here, give——
(*He dispossesses the rattler, who bawls.*)

KATE: Now you've set her off. She doesn't *understand*.
(*Comforting.*) Come on, then. . . .

ALBERT: Well, see you later.

KATE: Where are you going?

ALBERT: Work.

KATE: It's your Saturday off.

24

ALBERT: No, it's my Saturday on.
KATE: Last Saturday was your Saturday on.
ALBERT: Well, I'll take two off in a row.

(*Cut in bridge.*)
Listen . . .
The hot sun makes you think of insects,
but this insect hum is the whole city
caught in a seashell. . . .
All conversation is hidden there,
among motors, coughing fits, applause,
screams, laughter, feet on the stairs,
secretaries typing to dictation,
radios delivering the cricket scores,
tapes running, wheels turning, mills grinding,
chips frying, lavatories flushing, lovers sighing,
the mayor blowing his nose.
All audible life in the vibration
of a hairdryer in the room below.
(*Painting.*)
Dip brush, slide, stroke,
it goes on as smooth and shiny
as my sweat. I itch.
Paint on my arm,
silver paint on my brown arm;
it could be part of the bridge.
(*Painting stops.*)
Listen. The note of Clufton is B flat.
The whole world could be the same.
Look down. Is it a fact
that all the dots have names?
(*Cut bridge.*)

KATE: Jack Morris is taking Maureen and little Leslie to Paris.
ALBERT: Who's Jack Morris?
KATE: Next door, Albert.
ALBERT: Oh yes. Who's Maureen?
KATE: Mrs. Morris.

ALBERT: So little Leslie would be their little girl.

KATE: It's a little boy.

ALBERT: Ah. Why are we talking about them?

KATE: They're going to Paris for a holiday. Where are we going?

ALBERT: When?

KATE: That's what I'd like to know.

ALBERT: What?

KATE: Don't you have a holiday?

ALBERT: Oh. I suppose I must. Everybody does. Yes, I expect Fitch took that into account.

KATE: You're not going to dodge your holiday—I know what you're up to, you're already working full Saturdays, don't think I'm such a fool that I don't know. . . . And you're working till dark.

ALBERT: Overtime. I lose time in the winter.

KATE (*sniffing*): It's because you don't like it here, being at home.

ALBERT: Oh, Kate . . . I've got a schedule, you see.

KATE: You're miles ahead of it.

ALBERT: I've got to have some in hand in case of accidents.

KATE: I told you! You'll fall off, and me and Katherine will be alone.

ALBERT: No, no, no . . . stop crying. We'll have a holiday. I'll take a week.

KATE: A fortnight.

ALBERT: All right, I don't mind.

KATE: Can we go to Paris?

ALBERT: I've been to Paris. There's nothing there, believe me. We could go to Scotland.

KATE: Touring?

ALBERT: Certainly. The Firth of Forth.

KATE: We haven't got a car. Maureen said we could go with them.

ALBERT: But they're going to Paris.

KATE: We could afford it. It wouldn't be hard, it's easier with two children and joined forces. . . . It would be lovely, I've always wanted to see the Champs Elysee and the Ark de Triumph and the Seine and the Eiffel Tower. . . .

26

(*Cliché French accordion music. Cross-fade to Eiffel Tower. It's the same as Clufton Bridge.*)

(*Distant. Shouting up.*) Albert! A-a-albert! (*Repeated, fading, despairing.*) Come down! Please come down!

ALBERT: I thought as much. Dots, bricks, beetles . . . in B flat. Still, I'm glad I came. The pointlessness takes one's breath away—a tower connects nothing, it stands only so that one can go up and look down. Bridge-builders have none of this audacity, compromise themselves with function. Monsieur Eiffel, poet and philosopher, every eight years I'll scratch your name in the silver of Clufton Bay Bridge.

KATE (*distant, despairing*): Al-bert!

ALBERT (*quiet*): Coming down.

(*Cut Eiffel Tower.*)

(*Crockery smashes, flung against wall.*)

KATE: What's her name?

ALBERT: Kate. . . .

KATE: What a bloody coincidence!

ALBERT: You've got it all wrong, Kate, there's no woman——

KATE (*crying*): I can smell her on your coat!

ALBERT: It's paint—I tell you I was up on the bridge.

KATE: All night!

ALBERT: I just thought I would. It was nice up there.

KATE: You're barmy if you expect me to believe that, you're round the twist——

ALBERT: It's true——

KATE: And I believe it, I *am* round the twist! I'm as barmy as you are, but I believe it——

ALBERT: That's better——

(*Another cup smashes.*)

KATE: No it isn't—it's worse! A woman would be normal. (*Breaking down.*) You don't talk to me, you don't talk to Katherine, you can't wait to get out of the house and up your favourite girder. (*Quieter, sobbing.*) You don't like me any more, I know you don't—I'm boring for you, I haven't got what you want, and you don't want to hear the things

27

I tell you because I've got nothing to tell you, nothing happens. . . .

ALBERT: I like a quiet life, that's all.

KATE: Gutless. You'll spend your whole life painting that bridge. . . .

ALBERT: It's a good job.

KATE: You know damn well it's a stupid job which any thick idiot could do—but you're educated, Albert. You had opportunities. There was Metal Alloys and Allied Metals—you could have gone right up the ladder—we'd have a house, and friends, and we'd entertain and Katherine would have nice friends—you could have been an executive!

ALBERT: I was lying in bed one day when the maid came in to make it. . . . She was all starchy. When she moved, her skirt sort of crackled against her nylons. . . . I never had any regrets, but I did want her to be happy too.

KATE (*sobbing*): I've begun talking to myself, over the sink and stove. . . . I talk to myself because nobody else listens, and you won't talk to me, so I talk to the sink and the stove and the baby, and maybe one day one of them will answer me.

(*Baby gurgles, almost a word.*)

(*Cut to bridge and painting.*)

ALBERT (*crooning flatly amid and around the tune of 'Night and Day'*):
Night and day, I am the one . . .
day and night, I'm really a part of me. . . .
I've got me under my skin.
So why
don't I take all of me
When I begin the beguine. . . .
I get accustomed to my face,
The thought of me makes me stop
before I begin
Yes, I've got me under my skin,
and I get a kick out of me. . . .

28

Day and night, night and day. . . .
Shall I compare me to a summer's day,
'Cos I can't get me out of my mind
I saw me in Monterey . . .
and I'm all right by me,
yes I'm all right, I'm all right,
I'm all right by me. . . .
(*Applause, two-handed, from quite close. Painting stops.*)
Who's there? Who's that?

FRASER (*applauding*): Very nice, very nice. The egotist school of
   songwriting.

ALBERT: Who are you?

FRASER: You mean my name?

ALBERT: I suppose so.

FRASER: Fraser.

ALBERT: What are you doing on my bridge?

FRASER: Yours?

ALBERT: I'm painting it. I'm authorized.

FRASER: You've got a big job ahead of you.

ALBERT: I've got the time.

FRASER: You've got the time perhaps, but I'd say that time is
   against you. The condition of the paintwork is very
   shoddy.

ALBERT: Well, it hasn't been done for a fair while.

FRASER: Yes, it's beginning to look definitely tatty.

ALBERT: I'm getting through it bit by bit.

FRASER: Too slow. The old paint isn't lasting. People have
   noticed, you know. There's been talk.

ALBERT: Look here—are you the bridge inspector or something.

FRASER: What?

ALBERT: Did Mr. Fitch send you?

FRASER: Who?

ALBERT: What's it all about then?

FRASER: Look down there. I came up because up was the only
   direction left. The rest has been filled up and is still filling.
   The city is a hold in which blind prisoners are packed wall
   to wall. Motor-cars nose each other down every street, and
   they are beginning to breed, spread, they press the people

29

to the walls by their knees, pinning them by their knees, and there's no end to it, because if you stopped making them, thousands of people would be thrown out of work, and they'd have no money to spend, the shopkeepers would get caught up in it, and the farms and factories, and all the people dependent on them, with their children and all. There's too much of everything, but the space for it is constant. So the shell of human existence is filling out, expanding, and it's going to go bang.

ALBERT: You're frightened of traffic?

FRASER: We are at the mercy of a vast complex of moving parts, any of which might fail. Civilization is in decline, and the white rhino is being wiped out for the racket in bogus aphrodisiacs.

ALBERT: An animal lover——

FRASER: That was merely a trifle I snatched at in my inability to express the whole. I have never been able to understand, for instance, why anyone should want to be a dentist. I cannot pin down the divinity which ensures that just so many people take up dentistry and just so many agree to milk the cows which would otherwise scream in pain just as children would scream if there were no dentists.

ALBERT: I see. A lunatic, in fact.

FRASER: Not certifiably so. By no means certified. I am simply open, wide open, to certain insights. I do not believe that there is anyone in control. There is the semblance of pattern—supply meeting demand, one-way streets, give and take, the presumption of return tickets, promises to pay the bearer on demand, etcetera—but there's nothing really holding it together. One is forced to recognize the arbitrariness of what we claim to be order. Somewhere there is a lynch pin, which, when removed, will collapse the whole monkey-puzzle. And I'm not staying there till it happens.

ALBERT: I see. Well, we all have our problems, but I don't see how that justifies you climbing about council property. So would you kindly descend——

FRASER: That's what I came up for.

ALBERT: To descend?

FRASER: It never occurred to me to stay.

ALBERT: You came up to go down?

FRASER: To jump.

ALBERT: Jump?

FRASER: Off.

ALBERT: Jump off? You'd kill yourself. Ah.

FRASER: Yes.

ALBERT: I see. All right, then.

FRASER: My mind was made up——

ALBERT: I see your point.

FRASER: It seemed the easiest thing to do.

ALBERT: I agree. Well then, time is hurrying by, waiting for no man. Or is that tide?

FRASER: I see you're trying to humour me. Well, I expected that. You'll be sending for a priest next.

ALBERT: Come, come, don't procrastinate.

FRASER: Me?

ALBERT: You said you were going to jump.

FRASER: Well?

ALBERT: Well, jump.

FRASER: Aren't you going to try to talk me out of it?

ALBERT: You know your own mind. And you're holding me up. I've got to paint where you're standing.

FRASER: You wouldn't just stand there without lifting a finger?

ALBERT: I knew it. You're just a talker. Those ones never do it.

FRASER: I can't believe it. You wouldn't just stand there and watch me kill myself.

ALBERT: I thought that's what you wanted.

FRASER: Well, I did. I couldn't bear the noise, and the chaos. I couldn't get free of it, the enormity of that disorder, so dependent on a chance sequence of action and reaction. So I started to climb, to get some height, you know, enough height to drop from, to be sure, and the higher I climbed, the more I saw and the less I heard. And look now. I've been up here for hours, looking down and all it is, is dots and bricks, giving out a gentle hum. Quite safe. Quite

31

small after all. Quite ordered, seen from above. Laid out
in squares, each square a function, each dot a functionary.
I really think it might work. Yes, from a vantage point
like this, the idea of society is just about tenable.

ALBERT: Funked it. Well, mind how you go. Don't fall.

(*Cut bridge.*)

CHAIRMAN: Gentlemen. This special emergency meeting of the
Clufton Bay Bridge Sub-Committee has been called as a
result of public representations, both direct and via the
press, concerning the unsightly condition of what is the
symbol of Clufton's prosperity. My grandfather, who was
loved by the public, and owed everything to them, must be
turning in his grave. It is a salutary reminder that we are all
servants of the public, Mr. Fitch.

DAVE: Hear hear, Mr. Chairman.

CHAIRMAN: Shut up, Dave. As chairman, I, of course, take full
responsibility. That is the duty of the chairman, regardless
of where that responsibility actually lies, Mr. Fitch.

GEORGE: Hear hear, Mr. Chairman.

CHAIRMAN: It is no smiling matter, George. The city publicity
officer has been on to me, the Parks and Amenities have
been on to me, British Railways have been on to me and
the *Clufton Chronicle* has been doing its damndest to get on
to me. This committee is the shame and the laughing stock
of the Clufton Council, and as the future—as a possible
future Mayor, I am gravely embarrassed by having to carry
the can for a lack of foresight and watchfulness on the part
of committee members whose names I will not mention,
George. I have issued a statement to the effect that the
squalid state of disrepair of Clufton's highly-respected
bridge is the result of a miscalculation by a senior public
official, for which I, as chairman, take full responsibility,
Mr. Fitch.

FITCH (*a broken man*): I can only say in mitigation that I have
been under pressure—a sick man—domestic and financial
worries——

CHAIRMAN: Quite, quite. Let's stick to essentials. Two years ago,

32

at your insistence and against my better judgement, which
I left unspoken in deference to your professional capacity,
we arranged to switch to improved paint lasting eight
years, and through a reasoning which I never pretended
to follow, to sack three of the four painters. Today, two
years later, we are left with a bridge that is only one
quarter painted while the other three-quarters is in a
condition ranging from the sub-standard to the decrepit.
Now then—what happened?

FITCH: Mr. Chairman, gentlemen, I have served Clufton man
and boy for five years. . . . Clufton is the repository of
my dreams and boyhood memories, the temple of my hopes
to transform the running of a living community to a thing
of precision and efficiency, a cybernetic poem—a pro-
grammed machine as perfect as a rose——

CHAIRMAN: For God's sake, Fitch, pull yourself together.

FITCH: Gentlemen, let us take as our starting point the proposi-
tion that X painters painting at the rate of Y would take Z
years to paint surface ABC. We found that when X equalled
four, Z equalled two, Y and ABC remaining constant.
Then along came factor P, a paint lasting eight years——

CHAIRMAN: I can't stand it.

GEORGE: I think what Mr. Fitch is getting at Mr. Chairman is
that the brown paint on the bridge was only supposed to
last two years, the time that it took four painters to finish
the job and start again. Well, of course, when we cut down
to one painter using eight-year paint, it was obvious that
in two years' time he'd only be a quarter of the way along,
so the old paint would be ready for another coat.

CHAIRMAN: If it was obvious why didn't you say so?

GEORGE: I couldn't catch the eye of the chairman. Of course, if
we could hang on for another six years, Mr. Fitch would
emerge triumphantly vindicated as the poet of precision
and efficiency.

CHAIRMAN: I might be dead in six years.

DAVE: Hear hear, Mr. Chairman.

CHAIRMAN: Thank you, Dave. So what are we going to do
about it? Fitch?

C   33

FITCH: Er. . . . If we hired extra painters, one to start at the far end, one in the middle going one way, another going the opposite way, no . . . er, the progressive element intercedes —if we have two painters back to back at a point nine-sixteenths from the far end—no——

CHAIRMAN: We'd better go back to the old system and hire three more painters. Carry on from there.

FITCH: You can't do that! They wouldn't be quick enough on the one hand and they'd finish too soon on the other—you see, the bridge won't need re-painting for another six years, and the resultant coefficient—waste and unsightliness—the entire system would disintegrate and cost thousands——

CHAIRMAN: Money? (*Appalled.*) My grandfather——

GEORGE: I think I see a way out, Mr. Chairman. From the points of view of efficiency and expediency, I think we can get the whole thing resolved with just a bit of organization.

FITCH: Every day counts.

GEORGE: One day is all we'll need.

　(*Cut.*)

ALBERT: Met a feller up on the bridge the other day.

KATE (*strained*): Oh yes?

ALBERT: Yes. Climbed up to chuck himself off.

KATE: Did he?

ALBERT: No. Once he got up there, the mood passed.

KATE: Albert. . . .

ALBERT (*going*): Just off.

KATE: You used to say good-bye.

　(*Cut to bridge.*)

FRASER: Hello.

ALBERT: Who's that?

FRASER: Me again.

ALBERT: Did you forget something?

FRASER: No, it all came back to me. After I went down, it all started again. So I came back up.

ALBERT: To jump?

FRASER: Yes.

34

ALBERT: Go on then.

FRASER: I'm all right again now. I don't want to.

ALBERT: Now look here, this isn't a public right of way. I'll report you.

FRASER: I can't help it. I'm forced up and coaxed down. I'm a victim of perspective.

ALBERT (*shouts*): Get down!

FRASER: All right, I'm going.

(*Cut bridge.*)

ALBERT: I'm not a complaining man. I let people get on with their own lives, I'm sympathetic to problems, but a line must be drawn. I've found him up there four times now, Mr. Fitch, and each time it's the same story—he doesn't want to jump after all. I've given him every chance.

FITCH: Yes yes, but that isn't what I've asked to see you about at all. You haven't been listening to me.

ALBERT: It's unnerving me, finding company up there. Well, it's changing the character of the job, and playing hell with my schedule—simply on the level of efficiency I protest.

FITCH: Well, as I say, for the reasons given, the matter is to be resolved. We have to get the bridge finished by the end of the week.

ALBERT: What?

FITCH: We can't allow further deterioration. The public is roused.

ALBERT: Wait a minute—I can't possibly finish by the end of the week.

FITCH: I realize, of course, you'll need help. I have made arrangements.

ALBERT: What arrangements?

FITCH: Eighteen-hundred painters will report for work at seven o'clock tomorrow morning. By nightfall the job will be done. I have personally worked it out, and my department has taken care of the logistics.

ALBERT: Eighteen-hundred?

FITCH: Seventeen-hundred-and-ninety-nine. I kept a place for you. I thought you'd like that.

35

(Cut to door slam.)

ALBERT *(breathless)*: They're moving in on me, the dots are ganging up. I'll need food and spare clothes, a couple of blankets. What are you doing?

KATE *(off)*: Packing, Albert. I'm going.

ALBERT: Kate, they've got it in for me. They're trying to move me off—and I've earned my position. I've worked for it.

KATE *(approach)*: I've got a position—a housemaid, living in. With Katherine. I'll let you know my days off, for visiting. *(Pause.)*

ALBERT: Kate . . . I'm sorry. . . . Will you come and see me sometimes. . . . ? Will you come along and wave?

(Cut in bridge and painting.)
(More rapid than before.)
Dip brush, dip brush—slap it on, slide silver
over the iron, glide like mercury—slick, wipe
tickle it wet, swish, slop, sweep and wipe the
silver slime, it's all I can do—
in eight years I'll be pushing thirty-two
a manic painter coming through for the second time.
Dip brush, dip brush—

FRASER: What's the rush?

(Painting stops.)

ALBERT: Fraser.

FRASER: You're going at it.

ALBERT *(shouting)*: Get down! Get down!

FRASER: This isn't like you at all.

ALBERT: I'm not having you up here.

FRASER: There's room for both of us.

ALBERT: You're just the first, and I'm not going to have it. If you're going to jump—jump.

FRASER: That's why I came, again.

ALBERT *(closer and quieter)*: You're going to jump?

FRASER: No. Not today.

ALBERT *(furious)*: Up and down like a yo-yo!

FRASER: I agree that it is ludicrous. Down there I am assailed by the flying splinters of a world breaking up at the speed of procreation without end. The centre cannot hold and the outside edge is filling out like a balloon, without the assurance of infinity. More men are hungry than honest, and more eat than produce. The apocalypse cannot be long delayed.

ALBERT: You'd be better out of it. I'll tell them why you did it, if that's what worrying you.

FRASER: . . . So I climb up again and prepare to cast myself off, without faith in angels to catch me—or desire that they should—and lo! I look down at it all and find that the proportions have been re-established. My confidence is restored, by perspective.

ALBERT: But it's my bridge——

FRASER: You think only of yourself—you see yourself as the centre, whereas I know that I am not placed at all——

ALBERT: There are other bridges—bigger——

FRASER (*listening*): What's that?

ALBERT: San Francisco—Sydney——

FRASER: Listen.

ALBERT: Brooklyn—there's a place for you——

FRASER: Listen!

ALBERT: —but I was here first—this is mine——
(*He tails off as there is the faintest sound of 1,800 men marching, whistling 'Colonel Bogey'.*)

FRASER: There's an army on the march. . . .

ALBERT: So they're coming. . . .

FRASER: A solid phalanx moving squarely up the road, an officer at the head. . . .

ALBERT: Fitch.

FRASER: But they're not soldiers.

ALBERT: He's mad.

FRASER (*appalled*): They're just—people.

ALBERT (*shouts—to the people*): Go away!

FRASER: Coming here.

ALBERT: Halt! About turn!

FRASER: They've lined up hundreds and hundreds of ordinary people—the overflow—all the fit men in the prime of life —they're always the ones on the list—preference is given

37

to the old and the sick the women and children—when it comes to the point, it the young and able-bodied who go first——

ALBERT: Can't you see—they're taking over!

FRASER: Ten abreast—six y deep—and another phalanx behind —and another—successive waves——

(*The whistling is getting louder.*)

—so it has come to this.

ALBERT: They're going to come up!

FRASER: It was the only direction left.

ALBERT: They're going to wheel right——

FITCH (*distant*): Right—wheel!

ALBERT: Off the road and through the gate——

FITCH: Straighten up there!

ALBERT: Up to the end of the bridge, on to the tracks——

FRASER: That's it, then—they have finally run out of space, the edges have all filled out and now there is only up.

ALBERT: Eighteen-hundred men—flung against me by a madman! Was I so important? Here they come.

(*This is difficult; as the front rank reaches the bridge, the tramp-tramp of the march should start to ring hollow, progressively as more and more leave terra firma and reach the bridge.*)

(*From now, approaching tears.*) I could have done it, given time——

FRASER: There will be more behind them—the concrete mixers churn and churn until only a single row of corn grows between two cities, and is finally ground between their walls. . . .

ALBERT: They didn't give me a fair chance—I would have worked nights——

FRASER: They'll all come following—women and children too— and those that are at the top will be pushed off like disgraced legionaires——

ALBERT: I had it under control—ahead of schedule——

FRASER: Ah well. But they should be breaking step.

(*Tramp tramp.*)

Like soldiers do when they come to a bridge——

38

ALBERT: I was all right—I was doing well——

FRASER: For the very good reason—
(*Tramp tramp.*)
that if they don't—

ALBERT: I was still young—fit—

FRASER: —the pressures cannot bounce—but build and have to break out—
(*The rivets are starting to pop.*)

ALBERT: —good head for heights——

FRASER: —they don't know, or don't believe it, but the physical laws are inviolable—
(*Cracking and wrenching.*)

ALBERT: What's happening?

FRASER: —and if you carry on like that, a bridge will shiver, the girders tensed and trembling for the release of the energy being driven through them—

ALBERT: —it's breaking up!

FRASER: —until the rivets pop—

ALBERT (*screams*): What are they doing to my bridge!

FRASER: —and a forty-foot girder moans like a Jew's harp—
(*Twang.*)
—and one's enough——

ALBERT: To go to such lengths! I didn't do them any harm! What did I have that they wanted?
(*The bridge collapses.*)

IF YOU'RE GLAD I'LL BE FRANK

From her first words it is apparent that GLADYS *is the* "TIM" *girl, and always has been.*

As such, she has two columns to herself.

The right-hand column is for the Speaking Clock, and as such it is ostensibly continuous. But of course we hear her voice direct, not through a telephone unless otherwise indicated.

The left-hand column is for her unspoken thoughts, and of course this one has the dominant value.

It should be obvious in the script when her "Tim" voice is needed in the background as counterpoint, and when it should be drowned altogether by the rising dominance of her thoughts.

When her "TIM" voice intrudes again I have indicated this not by the actual words she uses, because the actual time she announces should be related to the number of minutes or seconds that have passed (i.e. depending on the pace of the broadcast) but by suggesting the space of time *that her speaking voice should take up, and this appears in the script in this form: (3–4 seconds).*

GLADYS *operates the pips too, and these are indicated thus:* (PIP PIP PIP).

Some of GLADYS's *sustained passages fall into something halfway between prose and verse, and I have gone some way to indicate the rhythms by line-endings, but of course the effect should not be declamatory.*

Scene 1

FRANK, *who turns out to be a bus driver, is heard dialling* "TIM".

> GLADYS (*through phone*): At the
> third stroke it will be eight
> fifty-nine precisely.

FRANK (*amazed disbelief*): It can't be. . . .

(PIP PIP PIP.)

. . . At the third stroke it will be eight fifty-nine and ten seconds. . . .

(PIP PIP PIP.)

(*Fearful hope*): It's not. . . ?

. . . At the third stroke it will be eight fifty-nine and twenty seconds. . . .

(PIP PIP PIP.)

(*Joy.*) It is! . . . *Gladys!* It's my Gladys!
(*Fade.*)

Scene 2

Exterior mid traffic, Big Ben begins its nine a.m. routine. Cut to interior: no traffic, Big Ben fainter.

PORTER (*murmurs*): Nine o'clock. Here we go.
  (*What happens is this:* MYRTLE, MORTIMER, COURTENAY-SMITH, SIR JOHN *and the* FIRST LORD OF THE POST OFFICE (LORD COOT) *enter from the street on the first, third, fifth, seventh and ninth strokes of Big Ben respectively* (*the second, fourth, sixth and eighth strokes being heard through the closed door.*) *Each opening of the door lets in traffic sound momentarily and amplifies Big Ben*)
  (*Street door.*)
PORTER: Morning, Mrs. Trelawney.
MYRTLE (*gay*): Hello, Tommy.
  (*And out through door.*)
  (*Street door.*)
PORTER: Morning, Mr. Mortimer.
MORTIMER (*tired*): Good morning, Tom.
  (*And out through door.*)
  (*Street door.*)

PORTER: Good morning, Mr. Courtenay-Smith.

C.-SMITH (*vague*): Morning, Mr. Thompson.

>   (*And out through door.*)

>   (*Street door.*)

PORTER: Good morning, Sir John.

SIR JOHN (*aloof*): Ah, Thompson. . . .

>   (*And out through door.*)

>   (*Street door.*)

PORTER: Good morning, my Lord.

1ST LORD: Morning, Tommy. (*Conspiratorial.*) Anything to report?

PORTER: All on schedule, my Lord.

1ST LORD: Jolly good.

>   (*Through door.*)

MYRTLE: Good morning, your Lordship.

1ST LORD: Good morning, Mrs. Trelawney.

>   (*Through door.*)

MORTIMER: Good morning, my Lord.

1ST LORD: Good morning, ah, Mortimer.

>   (*Through door.*)

C.-SMITH: Good morning, Lord Coot.

1ST LORD: Good morning, Mr. Courtenay-Smith.

>   (*Through door.*)

SIR JOHN: What ho, Cooty.

1ST LORD: Morning, Jack.

>   (*Through door.*)

BERYL: Good morning, sir.

1ST LORD (*startled*): Who are you?

BERYL: I'm new.

>   (*Pause.*)

1ST LORD: I thought I couldn't account for you. . . . New what?

BERYL: New secretary, sir . . . Miss Bligh. They sent me over from Directory Enquiries last night.

1ST LORD: I see. What happened to my old—to Miss—er——

BERYL: Apparently she cracked, sir, at 1.53 a.m. I came at once.

1ST LORD: That's the ticket. The Post Office never sleeps. Do you know the form round here?

ERYL: Well. . . .

ST LORD: Quite simple. I'm the First Lord of the Post Office, of course. I'm responsible for the lot, with special attention to the Telephone Services, which are as follows—write them down——

UMP—dial-the-Test-score.
SUN—dial-the-weather.
POP—dial-a-pop.
BET—dial-the-racing-results.
GOD—dial-the-Bible-reading.
EAT—dial-a-recipe.

And so on, with many others, including the most popular and important of them all—TIM, dial-the-speaking-clock. We can't afford to lose track of time, or we'd be lost. Now, you see, we must keep a continuous check on all of them, because if you don't keep an eye on them they slide back. The strain is appalling, and the staffing problems monumental.

Shall we start checking, then? To begin with, synchronize our watches, and then check with TIM—ready? I make it just coming up to nine two and forty seconds. . . .

Scene 3

Follows straight on with the Time signal (PIP PIP PIP).
Heard direct, i.e. not through phone, as is GLADYS now.

GLADYS:

. . . At the third stroke it will be nine two and fifty seconds. . . .
(PIP PIP PIP.)
. . . At the third stroke it will be nine three precisely.
(PIP PIP PIP.)

Or to put it another way, three minutes past nine, precisely, though which

nine in particular, I don't
say, so what's precise
about that? . . .

                    . . . nine three and ten
                    seconds. . . .
                    (PIP PIP PIP.)

The point is beginning to be
    lost on me.
Or rather it is becoming a
    different point.
Or rather I am beginning
    to see through it.
Because they think that
    time is something they
    invented,
for their own convenience,
and divided up into ticks
    and tocks
and sixties and twelves
and twenty-fours . . .
so that they'd know when
    the Olympic record has
    been broken
and when to stop serving
    dinner in second-class
    hotels,
when the season opens and
    the betting closes,
when to retire;
when to leave the station,
renew their applications
when their subscriptions
    have expired;
when time has run out.
So that they'd know how
    long they lasted,
and pretend that it matters,
and how long they've got,

as if it mattered,
so that they'd know that we
    know that they know.
That we know, that is.
That they know, of course.

And so on.

*(Faint time clock, 2–3
seconds.)*

Ad infinitum.

I used to say ad nauseum
but it goes on long after you
    feel sick.
And I feel sick.
When you look down from
    a great height
you become dizzy. Such
    depth, such distance,
such disappearing tininess so
    far away,
rushing away,
reducing the life-size to
    nothing—
it upsets the scale you live by.
Your eyes go first, followed
    by the head,
and if you can't look away
    you feel sick.
And that's my view of time;
and I can't look away.
Dizziness spirals up between
    my stomach and my head
corkscrewing out the stopper
But I'm empty anyway.
I was emptied long ago.

Because it goes on,

45

this endless dividing up into
    equal parts,
this keeping track—
because time viewed from
    such distance
etcetera
rushing away
reducing the lifespan to
    nothing
and so on—
(*Pause.*)
The spirit goes first, followed
    by the mind.
And if you can't look away
    you go mad.

(*Time clock, 2–3 seconds.*)

Scene 4

FRANK *dialling; excited, intense. Ringing tone breaks off.*
OPERATOR *is heard through phone.*

OPERATOR: Number please.
FRANK: Listen, do all you people work in the same building?
OPERATOR: This is the operator—can I help you?
FRANK: I want to speak to Gladys Jenkins.
OPERATOR: What's the number, please?
FRANK: She works there—she's in the telephones, you see.
OPERATOR: Hello, sir—operator here——
FRANK: I want to be transferred to Mrs. Jenkins—this is her
    husband.
OPERATOR: Mrs. Jenkins?
FRANK: Speaking clock.
OPERATOR: Do you want to know the time?
FRANK: No—I want my Gladys! What's her number?
OPERATOR: Speaking clock?

FRANK : Yes.

OPERATOR : TIM.

FRANK : Her *number*.

OPERATOR : T-I-M.

FRANK : I demand to speak to your superior——

OPERATOR : Just a moment, sir, putting you through.

GLADYS (*through phone*) : . . . At the third stroke it will be nine twelve and forty seconds. . . .

FRANK : It's all right, Glad—it's me again—Frank!

(GLADYS's *timespeak continues underneath.*)

Can you hear me now, Glad?—I've had a time of it I can tell you—I must say, you gave me a turn! So that's where you got to—Gladys? Give over a minute, love—it's Frank—— Can you hear me, Gladys? Give me a sign?

(*Pause; timeclock.*)

I know your voice—it's you, isn't it Gladys—are they holding you?—I'll get you out of there, Gladys—I'll speak to the top man—I'll get the wheels turning, Gladys! I'll pull the strings, don't you worry, love—— But I've got to dash now, love—I'm calling from the terminus and we're due out——

(IVY, *a bus conductress breaks in.*)

IVY : Frank *Jenkins!* The passengers are looking at their watches!

FRANK (*to* IVY) : Just coming. (*To* GLADYS.) That was Ivy, my conductress—you don't know Ivy—I'm on a new route now, the 52 to Acton—— Keep your chin up, Glad—you can hear me can't you? I'll be giving you another ring later—— Good-bye, Gladys—oh, Gladys—what's the time now?

GLADYS : Nine fourteen precisely——

FRANK : Thanks, Glad—oh, *thank* you, Gladys! (*He rings off.*)

IVY (*off*) : Frank—it's nine fourteen—remember the schedule!

FRANK (*going*) : Hey, Ivy—I've found her—I've found my Gladys!

Scene 5

GLADYS (*direct voice now*):

> . . . At the third stroke
> it will be nine fourteen
> and twenty seconds. . . .
> (PIP PIP PIP.)

. . . At the third stroke . . .
I don't think I'll bother, I
don't think there's any point.
Let sleeping dogs and so on.
Because I wouldn't shake it off
~~by going back, I'd only be in~~
the middle of it,
with an inkling of infinity,
the only one who has seen both
    ends
rushing away from the middle.
You can't keep your balance
    after that.
Because they don't know what
    time is.
They haven't experienced the
    silence
in which it passes
impartial disinterested
godlike.
Because they didn't invent it at all.
They only invented the clock.
And it doesn't go tick
and it doesn't go tock
and it doesn't go pip.
It doesn't go anything.
And it doesn't go anything for
    ever.
It just goes,
before them, after them, without
them,

above all without them,
and their dialling fingers,
their routine-checking, schedule-
    setting time-keeping clockwork—
luminous, anti-magnetic,
fifteen-jewelled self-winding,
grandfather, cuckoo, electric
shock-, dust- and waterproofed,
    chiming;
it counts for nothing against the
    scale of time,
and makes them tiny, bound and
    gagged to the minute-hand
as though across a railway line—
struggling without hope, eyes busy
    with silent-screen distress
as the hour approaches—the express
swings round the curve towards
    them
(and the Golden Labrador who
    might have saved them
never turns up on time).

(2–3 seconds.)

And they count for nothing
    measured against
the moment in which a glacier
    forms and melts.
Which does not stop them from
    trying
to compete;
they synchronize their watches,
count the beats,
to get the most out of the little
    they've got,
clocking in, and out,
and speeding up,
keeping up with their time-tables,
and adjusting their tables to keep

up with their speed,
and check one against the other
and congratulate each other—
a minute saved to make another
   minute possible somewhere else
to be spent another time.
Enough to soft-boil a third of an egg:
hard-boil a fifth.

                          Precisely. . . .
                          (PIP PIP PIP.)
                          (*3–4 seconds.*)

Of course, it's a service if you like.
They dial for twenty second's worth
   of time
and hurry off contained within it
until the next correction,
with no sense of its enormity, none,
no sense of their scurrying
   insignificance;
only the authority of my voice,
the voice of the sun itself,
more accurate than Switzerland—
definitive
divine.

                     (*2–3 seconds, very faint.*)

If it made a difference
I could refuse to play,
sabotage the whole illusion
a little every day if it made a
   difference,
as if it would, if I coughed or
   jumped a minute
(they'd correct their watches by my
   falter).
And if I stopped to explain
At the third stroke it will be   At the third stroke it
                             will be. . . . (*Continues
                             3–4 seconds.*)

too late to catch up, far
far too late, gentlemen. . . .
they'd complain, to the Post Office
And if stopped altogether,
just stopped, gave up the pretence,
it would make no difference.
Silence is the sound of time passing.

(1–2 seconds, faint.)

Don't ask when the pendulum
   began to swing.
Because there is no pendulum.
It's only the clock that goes tick
   tock
and never the time that chimes.
It's never the time that stops.

(1–2 seconds, quick fade.)

Scene 6

VOICE THROUGH PHONE: . . . thirty minutes in a Regulo 5 oven
   until it is a honey coloured brown. . . . Serves six.
1ST LORD *(ringing off)*: Well, that's that one. Next.
BERYL: That was the last one, sir.
1ST LORD: Then start again at the beginning—continuous
   attention, you see. You'll have to take over this afternoon
   —I have a board meeting.
BERYL: Very good, sir.
1ST LORD: You don't have to call me sir. Call me my Lord.
BERYL: Very good, my Lord.
   (Phone rings.)
   Hello?
FRANK *(through phone)*: This is Frank Jenkins.
BERYL: Yes?
FRANK: It's about my wife.
BERYL: Yes?
FRANK: Is she there?

BERYL: This is the First Lord's office.

FRANK: I want the top man in speaking clocks.

BERYL: What name please?

FRANK: Jenkins—it's about my wife, Gladys. She's the speaking clock.

BERYL: Hold on, please.
My Lord, it's a Mr. Jenkins—he says his wife is the speaking clock.

1ST LORD: How extraordinary. Tell him we don't know what he's talking about.

Scene 7

GLADYS (*direct*):   . . . At the third stroke
                                       it will be eleven thirty
                                       precisely. . . .
                                       (PIP PIP PIP.)

Old Frank. . . .
Yes, we met dancing, I liked him
    from the first.
He said, "If you're Glad
I'll be Frank. . . ."
There was time to laugh then
but while I laughed a bumblebee
fluttered its wings a million times.
How can one compete?
His bus passed my window twice a day,
on the route he had then,
every day, with a toot and a wave
    and was gone.
toot toot toot
everything the same
if only you didn't know,
which I didn't
which I do.
He took his timetable seriously,
    Frank.

52

You could set your clock by him.
But not *time*—it flies by
unrepeatable
and the moment after next the
    passengers are dead
and the bus scrap and the scrap dust,
caught by the wind, blown into the
    crevasse
as the earth splits and scatters
at the speed of bees wings.
Old Frank. He had all the time
in the world for me,
such as it was.

                        (PIP PIP PIP.)

Scene 8

In the street FRANK'*s bus comes to a rather abrupt halt, the door of his cab opens, slams shut as he runs across the pavement and through a door. He is breathless and in a frantic hurry.*

FRANK: Hey, you—who's in charge here?

PORTER: I am. Is that your bus?

FRANK: Who's the top man—quick!

PORTER: You can't park there after seven if the month's got an R in it or before nine if it hasn't except on Christmas and the Chairman's birthday should it fall in Lent.

FRANK: I have an appointment with the chairman.

PORTER (*to the sound of horns*): Seems to be a bit of a traffic jam out there.

FRANK: What floor's he on?

PORTER: He's not on the floor this early. Is this your conductress?

(*As the door flies open.*)

IVY: Frank—what are you doing!

FRANK: All right, all right! (*To* PORTER.) Listen—I'll be passing your door again at one-fourteen. Tell him to be ready——

53

CONDUCTRESS: Frank—we'll get behind time!
FRANK (*Leaving hurriedly*): It's all right, I got ninety seconds
ahead going round the park. . . .
(*And out; and break.*)

Scene 9

In the street FRANK'*s bus draws up once more; same slam, same
feet, same door, same frenzy.*

FRANK: Where is he? I've got ninety-five seconds.
2ND PORTER: Who?
FRANK: Who are you?
2ND PORTER: What do you want?
FRANK: Where's the other porter?
2ND PORTER: Gone to lunch—it's one-fourteen.
FRANK: Never mind him—where's the chairman?
2ND PORTER: They eat together.
(*Door crashes open.*)
CONDUCTRESS: Frank *Jenkins!*
2ND PORTER: Like brothers.
CONDUCTRESS: What about the schedule!?
FRANK (*to* PORTER): Listen—I'll be back here at two forty-
seven——
CONDUCTRESS (*almost in tears*): I ask you to remember the
schedule!
2ND PORTER (*as the horns sound*): Hello—is that your bus out
there?
FRANK (*leaving hurriedly*): Two forty-seven!—tell him it's about
Gladys Jenkins!

Scene 10

GLADYS (*through phone*): . . . three fourteen and twenty
seconds. . . .
(PIP PIP PIP.)

1ST LORD (*ringing off*): Precisely! Next!

BERYL: God, my Lord.

GOD (*through phone*): In the beginning was the Heaven and the
Earth. . . .
(*Fade.*)

Scene 11

GLADYS (*direct*):   . . . At the third stroke
it will be three fourteen
and fifty seconds. . . .

Check, check, check. . . .
One day I'll give him something
to check up for . . .
tick tock
tick tock
check check
chick chock
tick
you can check
your click clock
by my pip pip pip   (PIP PIP PIP.)
I never waver,
I'm reliable,
lord, lord,
I'm your servant,
trained,
precisely.   . . . precisely.
(*With a click* FRANK *is on the line.*)
(*We hear him, as* GLADYS *does, through the phone.*)

FRANK: Hello, Gladys—it's Frank. I bet you wondered where
I'd got to. . . . Well, I've had a bit of trouble getting hold
of the right man, you see, but don't you worry because the
next trip will give me the time—I'll be bang outside his
door slap in the middle of the rush hour so I'll have a
good four minutes—can you hear me, Gladys? . . .
(*Breaks a little.*)

55

Oh, Gladys—talk to me—I want you back, I'll let you do
anything you like if you come back—I'll let you be a nun,
if that's what you really want . . . Gladys? I love you,
Gladys——

Hold on, love, hold on a bit, and I'll have you out of
there. . . .

Got to go now, Gladys, Ivy's calling me, we're due out.
Bye bye . . . bye bye. . . . (*Rings off.*)

GLADYS:

I can hear them all
though they do not know enough to
speak to me.
I can hear them breathe,
pause, listen,
sometimes the frogsong of clockwindings
and the muttered repetition to the
nearest minute . . .
but never a question of a question,
never spoken,
it remains open, permanent,
demanding a different answer
every ten seconds.

Until Frank.
Oh, Frank, you knew my voice,
but how can I reply?
I'd bring the whole thing down with a cough,
stun them with a sigh. . . .
(*Sobbing a little.*)
I was going to be a nun, but they wouldn't have me
because I didn't believe, I didn't believe *enough*, that is;
most of it I believed all right, or was willing to believe,
but not enough for their purposes, not about him being
the son of God, for instance, that's the part that put paid
to my ambition, that's where we didn't see eye to eye.
No, that's one of the main points, she said, without that
you might as well believe in a pair of old socks for all the
good you are to us, or words to that effect. I asked her to

56

stretch a point but she wasn't having any of it. I asked her
to let me stay inside without being a proper nun, it made
no difference to me, it was the serenity I was after, that and
the clean linen, but she wasn't having any of that.
(*Almost a wail.*)
But it's not the same thing at all!
I thought it would be—peace!
Oh, Frank—tell them—
I shan't go on, I'll let go
and sneeze the fear of God into
their alarm-setting, egg-timing,
train-catching, coffee-breaking
   faith in
an uncomprehended clockwork—

yes, if I let go,
lost track
changed the beat, went off the rails—
cracked——

                         ... At the third stroke it
                         will be three eighteen
                         and ten seconds. . . .
                         (PIP PIP PIP.)

At the third stroke   At the third stroke
it will be   it will be
three eighteen and   three eighteen and
twenty seconds. . . .   twenty seconds. . . .
And so what?   (PIP PIP PIP.)

At the third stroke   At the third stroke
it will be   it will be
too late to do any good,   three eighteen and thirty
gentlemen——   seconds. . . .
                         (PIP PIP PIP.)
At the third stroke   At the third stroke. . . .
Manchester City 2,
Whores of Lancashire 43 for
seven declared

At the third stroke
Sheffield Wednesday will be cloudy
and so will Finisterre. . . .
(*The Queen.*) So a Merry Christmas
and God Bless you everywhere. . . .
And now the Prime Minister!:
Gentlemen, the jig is up—I have
given you tears. . . .
And now the First Lord!—
Don't lose your heads while all
about you on the burning deck. . . .
Oh—Frank! Help me! . . .

Scene 12

FRANK's *bus stops abruptly. Same place, same slam, same feet, same door, same frenzy.*

FRANK: Right, let's not waste time—where is she?
PORTER: State your business.
FRANK: I'm looking for my wife.
PORTER: Name?
FRANK: Jenkins—you know me.
PORTER: *Her* name!
FRANK: Sorry—Jenkins.
PORTER: Better. Your name?
FRANK: Jenkins.
PORTER: Relative?
FRANK: Husband.
PORTER: Holds water so far.
FRANK: I demand to see your superior.
PORTER: Name?
FRANK: Jenkins!
PORTER: No one of that name here.
FRANK: I see your game—a conspiracy, is it?
PORTER (*as the horns sound*): Is that your bus out there?

58

FRANK: I demand to speak to the chief of speaking clocks.

PORTER (*as the door bursts open*): Here she comes.

IVY (*conductress*): I'm not covering up for you again, Frank Jenkins!

PORTER: Hey—you can't go in there!

   (*Door.*)

MYRTLE: Hello.

FRANK: Where's the top man?

MYRTLE: Keep on as you're going.

   (*Door.*)

MORTIMER: Who are you?

FRANK: I want my wife!

MORTIMER: Now, look here, old man, there's a time and place for everything——

FRANK: I want her back!

MORTIMER: My dear fellow, please don't make a scene in the office——

FRANK: You're holding her against her will——

MORTIMER: I think that's for her to say. The fact is Myrtle and I are in love——

FRANK: I want my Gladys.

MORTIMER: Gladys? Isn't your name Trelawney?

FRANK: Jenkins—where's my Gladys?

MORTIMER: Gladys?

FRANK: My wife——

MORTIMER: Are you suggesting that a man of my scrupulous morality——

   (*Door.*)

MYRTLE: Darling, there's a bus conductress outside——

MORTIMER: Thank you, Mrs. Trelawney——

IVY (*desperate*): Frank!—the traffic is beginning to move!

FRANK: I demand to see your superior!

MORTIMER: You can't go in there!

   (*Door.*)

C.-SMITH: Yes?

FRANK: Are you the top man?

MORTIMER: Excuse me, Mr. Courtenay-Smith, this man just burst into——

IVY: Frank—I ask you to think of your schedule!

FRANK: Shut up! You there, are you the top man?

C.-SMITH: In my field, or do you speak hierarchically?

FRANK: I speak of Gladys Jenkins.

C.-SMITH: Not my field——

FRANK: You've got my wife——

MORTIMER: How dare you suggest that a man of Mr. Courtenay-Smith's scrupulous morality——

IVY: Frank! the passengers have noticed!
    (*Door.*)

C.-SMITH: Where's he gone?

MYRTLE: Darling, what's going on?

MORTIMER: Mrs. Trelawney, I must ask you to address me——

C.-SMITH: My God—the time-and-motion system won't take the strain!

IVY (*fading*): Fra-a-a-nk. . . !

Scene 13

GLADYS (*breaking down slowly but surely*):

At the third stroke
I'm going to give it up,
yes, yes . . . it's asking too much,
for one person to be in the know
of so much, for so many . . .
and at the third stroke
Frank will come
. . . Frank. . . .
I'm going to drop it now,
it can go on without me,
and it will,
time doesn't need me—
they think I'm time, but I'm
not—
I'm Gladys Jenkins and at the
    third stroke

At the third stroke it
will be four twenty-
three and ten
seconds. . . .

60

I'm going to cough,
sneeze
whisper an obscenity that will leave
ten thousand coronaries sprawled
across their telephone tables,
and the trains will run half empty
and all the bloody eggs will turn to
volcanic rock smoking in dry
   cracked saucepans
as soon as I shout—
Ship!
(a vessel)
*Pis*cine!
(pertaining to fishes)
*Fruc!*tuate
(fruit-bearing)
(*She giggles hysterically.*)
oh yes I will
and then they'll let me go
they'll have to
because Frank knows I'm here—
come on, please Frank, I love you
and at the third stroke I will
yes I will yes at the third stroke I
   will. . . .

Scene 14

1ST LORD: Well, gentlemen, in bringing this board meeting to a
close, and I'm sure you're all as bored as I am,
(*Chuckle chuckle, hear hear.*)
I think we must congratulate ourselves on the variety and
consistency of the services which we in the telephone office
have maintained for the public in the face of the most
difficult problems. I believe I'm right in saying that if the
last Test Match had not been abandoned because of the

rain, UMP would barely have lasted the five days, but all
was well as it happened, though the same rainy conditions
did put an extra strain on SUN our weather forecast
service. . . . I don't know if you have anything to add, Sir
John?

SIR JOHN: Well, Cooty—my Lord, that is—only to join with the
rest of the Board in heartily congratulating you on the
excellent report——

(*Hear hear hear hear.*)

1ST LORD: Thank you. Now is there any other business?

(*Door.*)

FRANK (*out of breath*): Where's Gladys Jenkins?!

1ST LORD: There you have me, gentlemen.

SIR JOHN: Point of order, my Lord.

1ST LORD: Yes, Jack?

SIR JOHN: I don't think this man——

FRANK: I'm not taking any more of this—where've you got my
Glad——

(*Door.*)

C.-SMITH: Forgive me, my Lord—this man is quite
unauthorized——

IVY: Frank, the passengers are rioting! All is lost!

MORTIMER: Now look here——

MYRTLE: Darling, do shut up!

FRANK: Damn you. What have you done with my wife?

SIR JOHN: Don't you come here with your nasty little
innuendoes, Trelawney—whatever you may have heard
about the Bournemouth conference, Myrtle and I——

IVY: The passengers are coming!

(FIRST LORD *gets quiet by banging his gavel.*)

(*Pause.*)

(*Noise of rioting passengers.*)

1ST LORD: Gentlemen—please! (*Pause.*) Now what's all the row
about?

IVY: It's the passengers, sir.

FRANK: Are you the top man?

1ST LORD: Certainly.

FRANK: What have you done with my Gladys?

MORTIMER: How dare you suggest that a man of the First Lord's scrupulous morality——

1ST LORD: Please, Mr. Mortimer, let him finish.

FRANK: She's the speaking clock.

1ST LORD: What do you mean? *TIM?*

FRANK: Gladys. Yes.

1ST LORD (*chuckling*): My dear fellow—there's no Gladys—we wouldn't trust your wife with the *time*—it's a machine, I thought everyone knew that. . . .

FRANK: A machine?

1ST LORD: He thought it was his wife!
(*General chuckles.*)
Wife . . . thought it was his wife! . . .

FRANK: It was her voice——

IVY: Oh, Frank—they wouldn't use your Glad for that. It's just the speaking clock——

FRANK: She was educated——

IVY: Oh Frank—come on, come on now, we'll be in awful trouble with the Inspector.

FRANK: But Ivy—she *talked* to me. . . .

IVY: She couldn't have done——

1ST LORD: She *talked* to you, my dear fellow?

FRANK: Well, not exactly. . . .

IVY: Of course she didn't. Come on, now. . . .

1ST LORD: That's it—back to your offices gentlemen. We must all make up for lost time.
(*General movement out.*)

FRANK: But she sounded like my Gladys. . . .

IVY: You'll have to go on looking, Frank. . . .
(FIRST LORD *alone.*)

1ST LORD: Dear me, dear me. . . .
(*Door.*)

BERYL (*urgent*): Sir!

1ST LORD: What is it, Miss Bligh?

BERYL: It's the speaking clock—I was just checking it and——

1ST LORD: All right—get me TIM, I'll see to it.

BERYL: Yes, my Lord. (*Dialling.*) She's on now, my Lord.

GLADYS (*through phone. Sobbing hysterically*): At the third

stroke it will be five thirty five and fifty seconds. . . .
(PIP PIP PIP.)

1ST LORD: Mrs. Jenkins. . . . This is the First Lord speaking.

GLADYS: At the third stroke it will be five thirty-six
precisely. . . .

1ST LORD: Mrs. Jenkins—pull yourself together, stop crying.
And you've lost forty seconds somewhere by my watch——

GLADYS: At the third stroke I don't know what time it is and I
don't care, because it doesn't go tick tock at all, it just
goes and I have seen—I have seen infinity!

1ST LORD: *Mrs. Jenkins!*

GLADYS (*sniffing*): I can't go on!

1ST LORD: Come on now, this isn't like you at all. Let's get
things back on the rails, hm? Think of the public, Mrs.
Jenkins. . . . Come on now . . . at the third stroke. . . .

GLADYS: At the third stroke. . . .

1ST LORD: It will be five thirty seven and forty seconds.
(PIP PIP PIP.)
Carry on from there. . . .

GLADYS: At the third stroke it will be five thirty-seven and
fifty seconds. . . .

1ST LORD: That's it—spot on Mrs. Jenkins. Control your voice
now.
(PIP PIP PIP.)

GLADYS: At the third stroke it will be five thirty-eight
precisely.

1ST LORD: Well done, Mrs. Jenkins. Well done—I'll check you
again within the hour, as usual. (*Rings off.*)

GLADYS (*direct now*):

He thinks he's God. . . .

At the third stroke it
will be five thirty-eight
and ten seconds. . . .
(PIP PIP PIP.)
At the third stroke. . . .
(*Fading out.*)